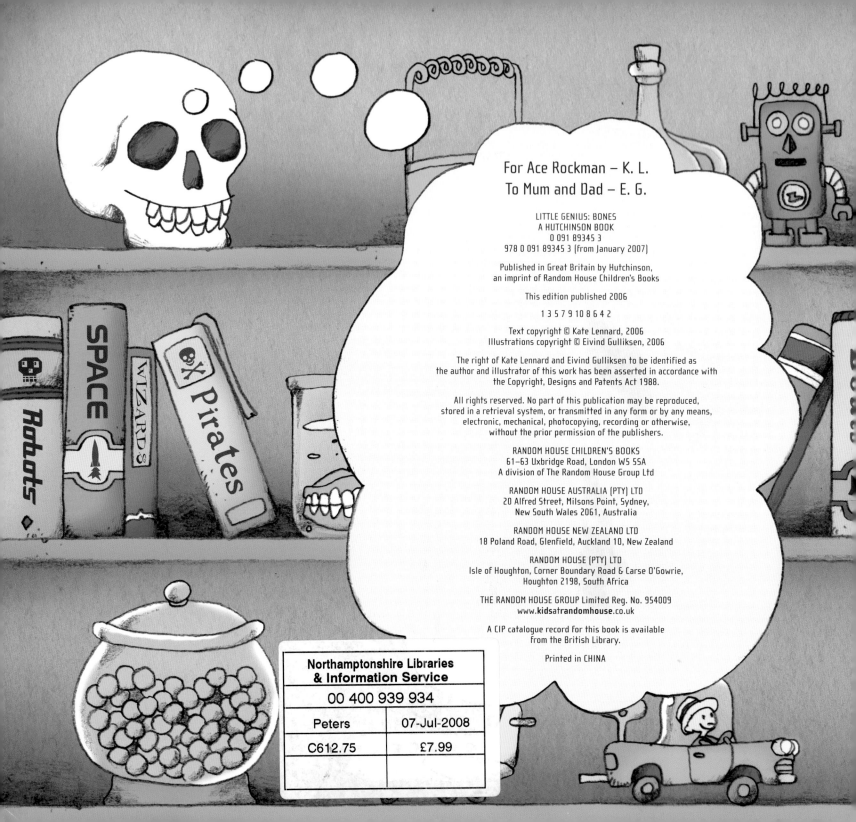

For Ace Rockman – K. L.
To Mum and Dad – E. G.

LITTLE GENIUS: BONES
A HUTCHINSON BOOK
0 091 89345 3
978 0 091 89345 3 (from January 2007)

Published in Great Britain by Hutchinson,
an imprint of Random House Children's Books

This edition published 2006

1 3 5 7 9 10 8 6 4 2

Text copyright © Kate Lennard, 2006
Illustrations copyright © Eivind Gulliksen, 2006

RANDOM HOUSE CHILDREN'S BOOKS
61–63 Uxbridge Road, London W5 5SA
A division of The Random House Group Ltd

RANDOM HOUSE AUSTRALIA (PTY) LTD
20 Alfred Street, Milsons Point, Sydney,
New South Wales 2061, Australia

RANDOM HOUSE NEW ZEALAND LTD
18 Poland Road, Glenfield, Auckland 10, New Zealand

RANDOM HOUSE (PTY) LTD
Isle of Houghton, Corner Boundary Road & Carse O'Gowrie,
Houghton 2198, South Africa

THE RANDOM HOUSE GROUP Limited Reg. No. 954009
www.kidsatrandomhouse.co.uk

A CIP catalogue record for this book is available
from the British Library.

Printed in CHINA

SPACE

WIZARDS

Pirates

Robots

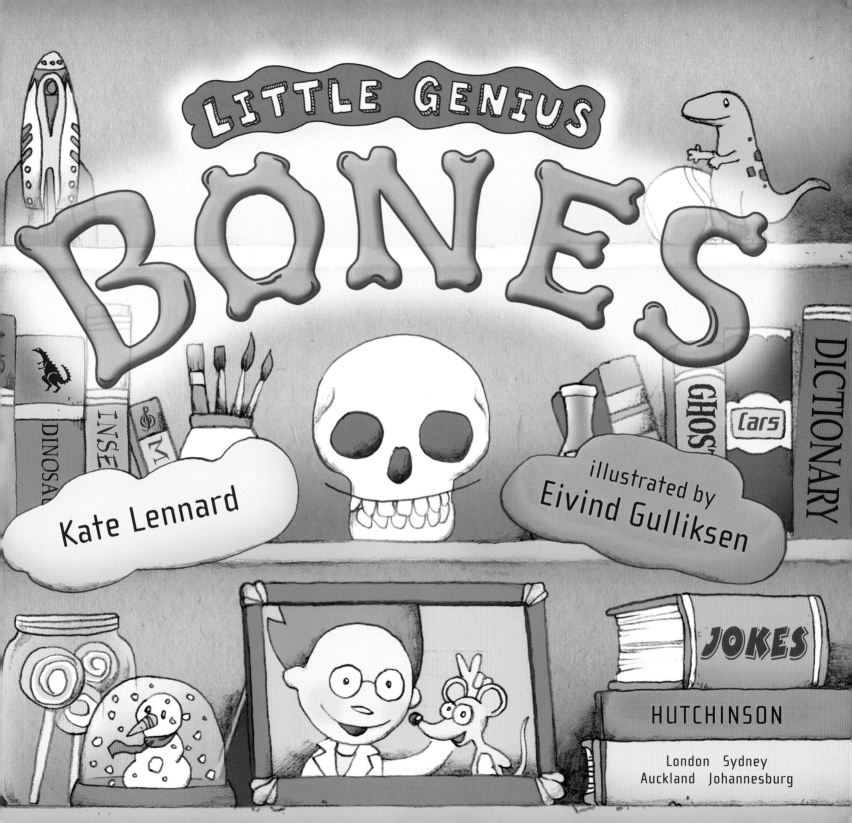

Hello!
I'm **Little Genius**.

I've been looking into the human body, and all the interesting bits that make it work.

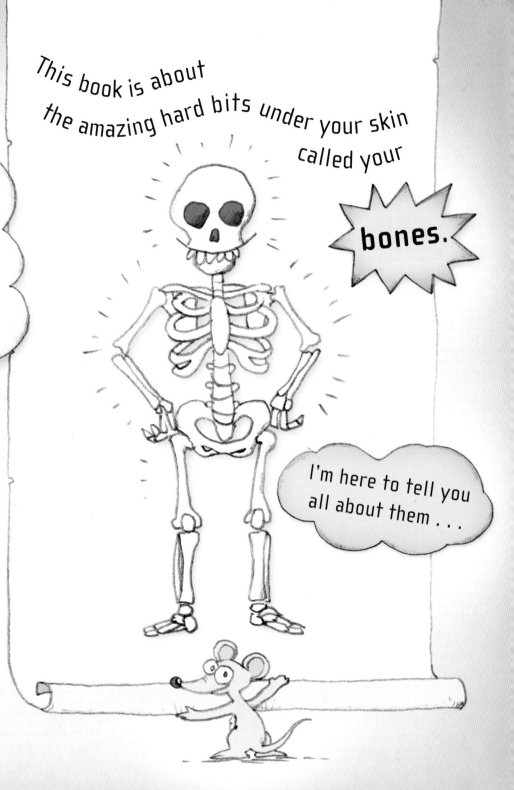

This book is about the amazing hard bits under your skin called your

bones.

I'm here to tell you all about them . . .

Inside your body,
under your skin,
is an amazing machine
called your
skeleton.

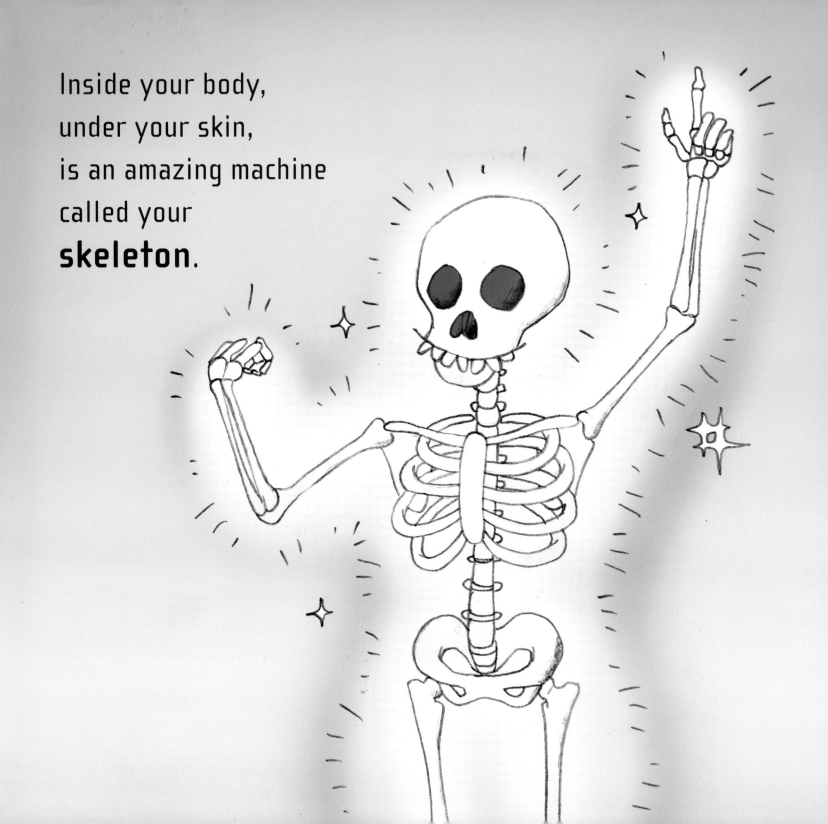

Your skeleton is made up of knobbly white sticks called **bones**.

And they fit together to make a frame that your insides can stick to.

Imagine that this lollipop is a person and the lollipop stick is the skeleton.

Take it away and you are left with a sticky mess.

This is what you'd be like if you didn't have any bones: a **splodge**!

Some bones are there to protect important squashy bits, like your **heart** and your **lungs**.

Your ribs make a strong, bony cage to keep them **safe**.

ribs

Can you find your ribs at your sides, above your tummy? They feel like the rungs of a ladder.

The bone inside
your head
is called
your **skull**.

skull

The skull is there to protect your brain.

Can you feel it in your head, like a helmet under the skin?

If it wasn't for your skull, your brain would slosh about inside your head, like a poached egg in a plastic bag.

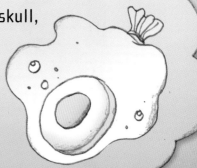

The pointy bone at your elbow is called your **funny bone**.

Ouch!

That's funny because when you bang it, it really hurts. And that's *not* funny.

The flat bone where your leg bends is called your **kneecap**.
It feels like a little plate over your knee.

And like a plate, your knee could smash into lots of pieces if you fell on it hard. And that would really hurt!

kneecap

That's why skaters wear knee pads.

There are three bones
in each of your fingers.
That's why they are
so bendy.

Your smallest bone
is in the **ear**.

Your longest bone
is in the **thigh**.

Having lots of finger bones means
that your hands can move around
and do fiddly things, like:

playing the piano.

Toes don't have as many
bones as fingers.
You can wiggle your toes,
but you can't write with your feet –
well, not without a lot of practice!

Bones are held together with special stretchy bits called **ligaments**. They're like elastic bands under the skin.

The place where two bones meet is called a **joint**.

ligaments

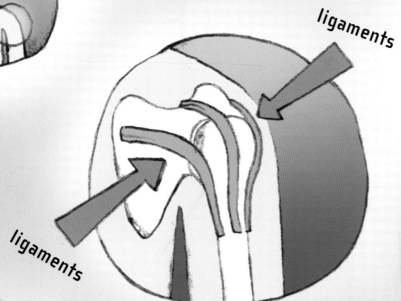

ligaments

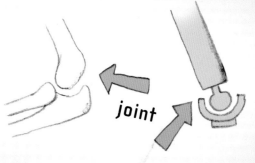

joint

Leg bones meet at the knee joint. They move backwards and forwards like a door.

Your legs are attached to your body at the hip joint. The joint moves around like a toffee apple cupped in the palm of your hand.

KAPOW!

Sometimes joints can get worn out. This old lady has been fitted with a robotic hip. Now she can do a karate kick!

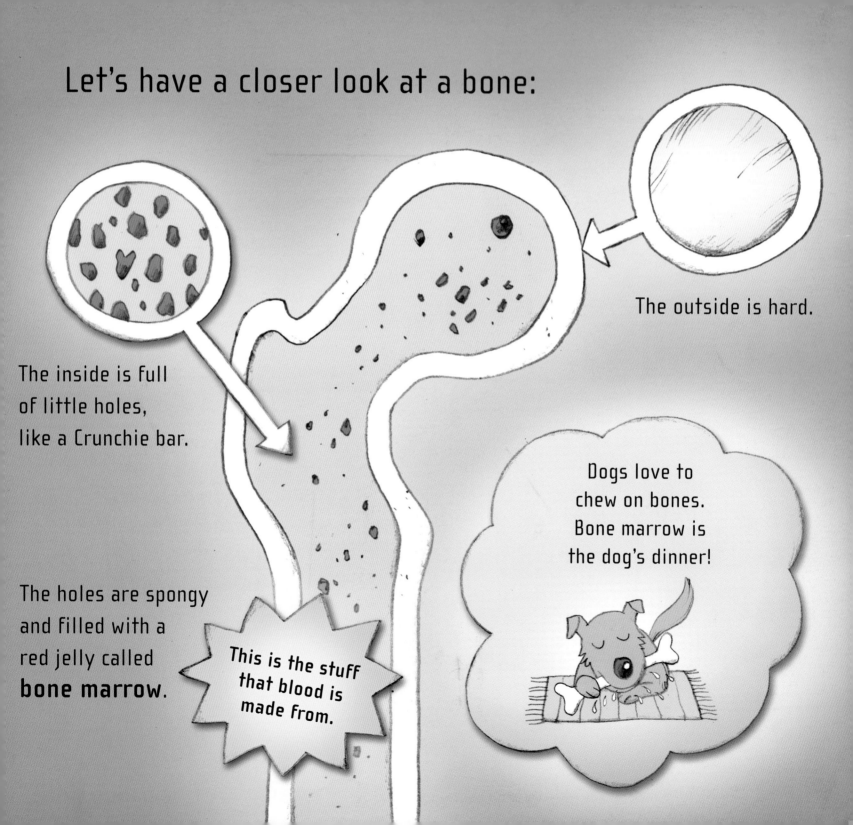

Let's have a closer look at a bone:

The outside is hard.

The inside is full of little holes, like a Crunchie bar.

The holes are spongy and filled with a red jelly called **bone marrow**.

This is the stuff that blood is made from.

Dogs love to chew on bones. Bone marrow is the dog's dinner!

Some creatures have bones sticking out of their heads.

This goat uses his big horns to show who's in charge.

C'MON, kids!

That moose has used his antlers to dig a big hole. And this poor deer has fallen in!

Some creatures don't have any bones at all, like:

Sharks
Their skeletons are made out of gristle, like the stuff you can feel when you press the end of your nose.

Jellyfish
They flubber about by opening and closing like an umbrella.

Slugs and worms
These creatures wriggle and slither along on muscle power.

They're aLL spineLess!

Some creatures, like insects and spiders, wear their bodies inside out!

Crabs and snails have exoskeletons called shells, for extra protection.

If this lobster got into a fight his bones would stop him from getting too badly hurt, like a knight wearing a suit of armour.

Eeeeeeek!

Exoskeletons are waterproof, like a raincoat. That's how this spider can keep popping back up the plughole.

It is possible to look at your bones without taking them out of your skin.

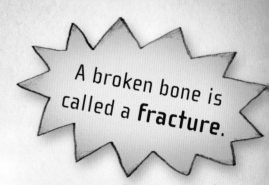

A broken bone is called a **fracture**.

A big machine can take a picture called an **X-ray**. A doctor may do this if he thinks that a bone is broken.

A small break is called a **hairline fracture**, meaning as thin as a strand of hair.

A **big** break means that the bone has snapped like a pencil!

If a bone is broken, it can mend itself.

Plaster cast

It's wrapped in a special bandage called a **plaster cast**. This will stop the bone from moving about so it can grow back together again.

It's a great surface for your friends to write their autographs on!

If a broken bone wasn't wrapped in a plaster cast, it might grow back in a funny position, like this!

Bones like food that contains calcium because it makes them strong.

yoghurt

rice

juice

cheese

milk

broccoli

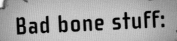
fish

exercise

Bad bone stuff:

not wearing helmets

no exercise

sitting still for too long

lifting heavy things

slouching

jumping without bending your knees

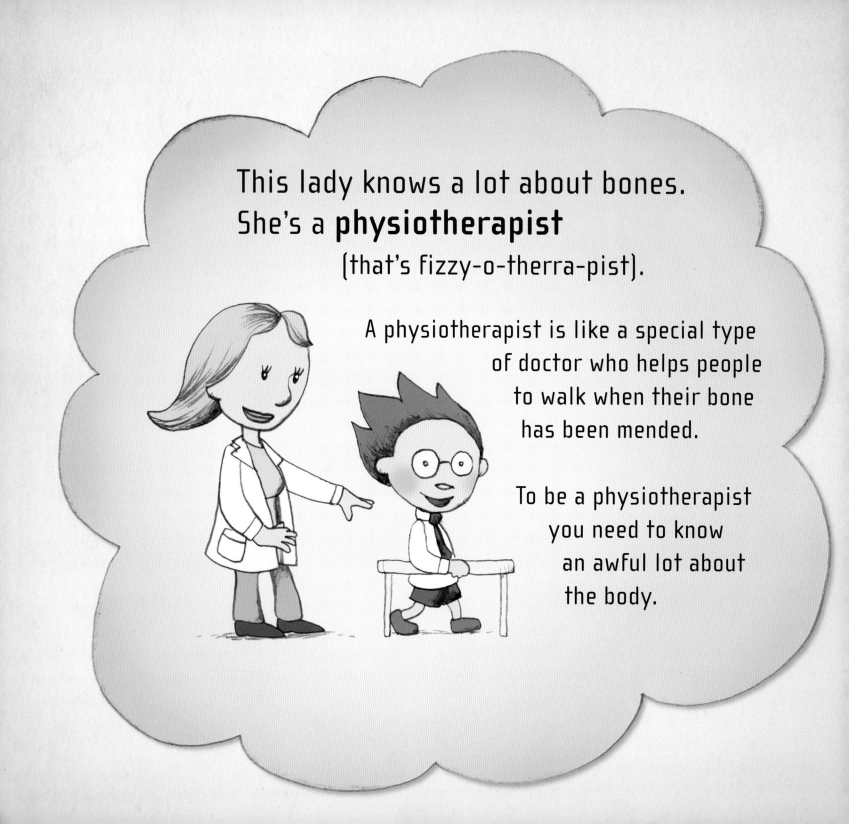

This lady knows a lot about bones. She's a **physiotherapist** (that's fizzy-o-therra-pist).

A physiotherapist is like a special type of doctor who helps people to walk when their bone has been mended.

To be a physiotherapist you need to know an awful lot about the body.

I'd like to be
a physiotherapist
when I grow up.

Would you?